Displacements

Poems by
Jean Rubin

DISPLACEMENTS

Copyright © 2008 by Jean Rubin.

Wildfire Poetry Press is an imprint of
Boudica Publishing Inc.
Allentown, PA

For sales, permissions, and all other inquiries, contact:
www.boudicapublishing.com

ISBN 0-9800549-0-7

Printed and bound in the United States of America.
First Edition

Acknowledgments

These pages of my work would never have been turned into a book but for the skills, the patience and the dedication of Liz Bradbury and Patricia Sullivan of Boudica Publishing. I am beholden to them – and grateful, too, for their friendship.

For Leonard Rubin
Brother, first and
truest friend

Contents

Ab Ovo

"I like to play with lizards,"
The long child said
When one came scuttling near.
She pressed and rubbed its skin—
"It's so tough and clean and dry"—
With her finger nail she flicked
A scale from behind its head,
Then sniffed her fingertip—
"It smells like yellow"—she gave
It a lick—"And tastes like egg
That's stale. I think his blood
Runs thick and cold and slow
So his quick, mad eyes
Can seize and set and hold—
Yet I can lock my eyes
To his and not be out-stared.
His kind reminds me of a world
Of wattled, pecking fowl,
Of gulls and ostriches and pelicans,
The buzzards and the songbirds, all.
And of that old woman
Who lived upstairs and stayed
All day in bed—her hand
With its thick sharp nails
Would dart from underneath the coverlet
To pinch and she would cackle
Whenever I would flinch."

But the girl will play with lizards
Only till summer comes;
In the slow and fertile heat
She will not need reminding
Of changes in the flesh that make it
Feather out—she'll go to bathe
Where leggy birds of passage
Take their stand and feed
On tadpoles and harmless snakes:
She'll peel her clothing off and let
The long silver strands
Of her hair web the surface of the lake.
When her hair turns green
She'll find she has become a woman
And wants to go where people are—
She'll finger cloth as women do,
Speak as women do to men
And hood her shimmering eyes
Beneath her heavy lids.
When her hair turns yellow
She'll bear a child and play,
Mindless of future and past
As she pinches the flesh of his thighs
And looks nakedly into his eyes.
When his strength is great enough
To break her grip and he runs,
She will laugh and let him go.

"With the short days of winter,"
The long child said,
"And the cold, I'll shrink into myself.
At last I'll remember everything,
And then forget it all again
For in spring I must be reborn,
Hatched from a yellow egg
With green and silver veins
And nestled in shimmering sands."

After Hafiz:
In Praise of Ardent Spirits

Meek until my moment came,
I raised the cup at last--but
What I drank I will not name--
Enough that, coursing gullet and gut,
It purges the spirit of guilt and shame.

Eyes that had been filmed with grime
And futile tears, peered through time--
Although I will not say how far
They searched, nor what pantomime
Beheld, nor what hurtling star—

And lips that had been stiff lest a word
That seemed unspeakable, be spoken,
Were at last by laughter stirred—
Although I kept my silence unbroken
And will not say what I found absurd—

(There are idols in bronze and stone
Of a god whose dance is said to shake
Life's dream—yet that dream was grown
And persists in the very bone—
Though bones, like the nerve, may break.)

4

And yet, spirits that quicken the mind—
Like fire, burning filth away,
Like winds, blowing fog away,
And tides, washing landmarks away—
Must be restrained, lest they blind.

After the Japanese

I.

At dusk we would heap
Sand castles, then watch the sea
Sweep them away—when,
Dear friend, from the farther shore
Of that sea, will you send word?

II.

The sheltered rose-bush—
Brief wealth of leaf and flower,
Subtlety of thorns—
Bemuses the wanderer
Who leans on a cane of ash.

III.

Brown bears in the park
Clown and clap for scraps to eat;
Tourists tease and laugh—
In dark forests, when the bear
Looms, what creature dares to breathe?

Andante Cantabile

Provocations: A said, plunge in icy currents
                  B said, sing

Sing, what shall I sing? That long ago
When libations ceased, Olympian Zeus
Whose voice the People heard as thunder,
Grew parched and finally mute; that now,
Where his temple used to be,
In a ruined, pock-marked stone
A little standing water breeds
Tiny snails and other sluggish things,
While in the grass between some columns
That remain and many fallen stones,
Pale moths and wildflowers blow
In the wind and the rain. Passing this way
A barbarian might linger long enough
To note that every dog has his day—
But here's stale matter for a song.

Then what shall I sing? Rain in Athens
Is no brighter than rain in London is,
Although the oranges are cheaper
And blaze along Athinas Street—
That gap-toothed crown, there,
Against the dark clouds, the Acropolis;
Here, the banks of oranges, gleaming eggplants,
Rows of apples, olives in barrels,

7

Festoons of sausage, ranks of cheese
And gypsy women, crouched and rummaging,
Bundled in rags, scowl, seem blind
To the milling crowd, deaf to the hawkers.
I've the Greek and the coin to get what I need
But a long way to go and shifting winds
At my back—I have no song for this.

In glancing sunlight, Grecian gulfs and seas
Achieve such molten blues as should,
Whoever plunged, wash away the wrangling hues
Of mind and flesh, or blend them into utter
Fluency—but the Attic air is binding
And I turn back along the road to Corinth,
Return to Athens and take once more
The stony path up to the Parthenon:
Despite the gaping foreigners and Greeks
And the rhetoric of their guides,
Despite the thrumming of the town below,
It is very quiet here—the Ancient Shield
Of Athens does not stir, nor am I moved,
Among such fragments, to break into song.

Once, in the course of travel,
I came to a promontory
Jutting into the sea and the sunset—
Where the land narrowed,
Across the rough path
That should have led

To the furthest point of land,
A seated figure loomed,
Backed by flaming clouds,
Blocking the sun
As the sun seemed to melt into the sea;
Her features were lost in the shadows,
In the deepening shadows
That anchored in earth the heavy,
The heaped folds of her garment—
But there must have been
Something like a smile on her lips,
And, over her eyes, heavy,
Deeply incised lids; her hands
Were large and her right hand
Was raised in a compelling gesture.
On the verge of an answering smile,
I drew back, turned away, and yet
Have been weighed down ever since
As if by a garment with many heavy folds
And since then have seen
As if from such depths that the shifting,
Even the icy currents seem
Mere stubborn streaks: such was the plunge
And hence, the density of my song.

So, if I am to sing,
It will not be
As birds sing, openly,
From their wicker or wire cages,

Or perched on the high,

The blossom laden branch

Of a fruit-bearing tree,

Who, captive or free-wheeling,

Sing, that is, sound, alike—

My song escapes

As from sealed lips,

A humming in spite of words,

In spite of a long thought,

A tone pitched like the pain

Of an ankle inadvertently turned

On broken pavements

Or on rock-strewn paths;

A sustained beat

Like the heaving of such a thought,

Such a sequence of thoughts,

Against the rib cage,

Like the laboring for breath

After a climb, near the summit

Of a long climb when, below,

The world is spread

In the deep glow of sunset,

But seen through a kind of mist

That sits upon the eyes

At the end of an endless climb.

Apery

Ape in a cage
Can imitate
The gaping public's ways:
Can dance.

Daily heaves against
Iron bars,
Works up sweat and frenzy,
Can't escape.

Bruised and spent,
Crouches trembling, spits.
The public laughs,
Not without sympathy.

Say, you bow-legged
Bent-shouldered creatures
Rocking back and forth
In cages,

Say where we are
That we are let kill
And be killed
And also let dance.

August

Pursued by eastern darkness, evening slips
Across the street and trails off in the west;
Now night prevails—and yet tomorrow clips
The stars and indiscreetly mars our rest;

This morning brings a hint of some bequest
That soon is baffled by the lidless stare
Of noon—the mind is held in stark arrest
While afternoon impassively lays bare

The massive grind and stint of daily care
Till twilight comes to pour her musty wine
And filter softened tones into the air—
Disarmed, we fall for her seductive line.

So nature does, by brutal means or fine,
Ensure that we are drawn to her design.

August #2

The year is big with summer:
Earth bears her ripening fruit
And burdens the air with gross humors;

Wind thickens sweating thighs;
Veins swell in the hands;
Speech lags and blurs;

Desires of the mind yield
To desires in the blood, and will
Yields to the welter of the season;

The spirit, caught in the toils
Of fertility, broods on death;
The word is made flesh.

Ballad

Only death shall end my folly,
　Come, oh lovely, come.
　　　　I gave to my love a dawdling time
　　　　With a cat that curled in the lap,
　　　　And a quaint old song made over to rhyme
　　　　And a bright new feather for's cap—
So come, my lovely, come
As only death can end my folly—
　　　　I gave to my love a chowder of fish
　　　　And for eating, a runcible spoon
　　　　And I read to him from my crystal dish
　　　　His chances as spelled by rune—
Only death shall end my folly,
　Come, oh lovely, come.
　　　　But heedless was he as a barking dog
　　　　That hankers for boundless sport,
　　　　And all folded round in a rag of fog
　　　　He blindly went to pay his court—
So come, my lovely, come
As only death can end my folly—
　　　　He kept the spoon and the feather atilt
　　　　But this was the catch in the game,
　　　　That silver must turn and a feather wilt
　　　　And emptiness stifle flame—
Only death shall end my folly,
　Come, oh lovely, come.

Birdscapes

(Pakistan)

All day long, eagles and kites
Circle the city—they soar,
Swoop and soar. In this tree,
In its bare upper branches,
Four vultures sit very still.
A flock of sparrows settles
On the ground, momentarily.

And the multitude of crows,
Crows as large as kettles,
Thriving on waste and carrion,
They swagger in street and field.
One, on the balcony railing,
Stands and squawks—black feathers
Have a blue sheen in the sunlight.

In the evening, parrots flash
Among the trees, parrots as green
As the leaves, shrieking as the sun
Sinks below the large horizon,
And the night watchman, summoned
Before his rounds begin, sings
A song welcoming the guest.

Blindman's Bluff

This stuff that comes to hand readily,
That is not stable, and when it ebbs
Leaves harsh distracting odors
Behind—this is, they say,
Bulky, gross, instructive.

        I would make a good juggler
        If my hands did not grow cold
        At the very thought. All I need
        Is fluid fingers, a dead eye
        And a head for geometry…

This stuff that comes readily to hand,
Staining the fingers yellow,
Thickly formulating effigies
That shift like unfinished structures
In the fog, but trickle away as well,

This stuff, they say, at something more
Than the instance of the simple heart,
Can be packed down tight, molded,
Made impermeable and left,
Preferably, at an intersection…

Once, unwitnessed, I held in play
Several objects of diverse dimensions;
It was splendid—I scarcely knew
What I was doing. But night came,
As night will, too soon.

Caliban's Reverie

If Ariel were bound again,
His wailing might splay the air,
Stay wind and tide,
Delay the cycles of the stars,
Stagger birds in flight,
Pacing thoroughbreds and goats
Prancing on the rocky heights.

(I am neither deaf nor blind—
Loveliness may be most compelling
To the gross: in still shadows
 I have felt a sudden rush
Of air, found light
But not its source and known
It was Ariel dancing, oblivious—
In dreams I reach out to him,
He takes my hand and joins me
To his dance—then, I wake up.)

Ariel, held down, would seem
Less than what he is, but more
Within my touch, and then I might
Catch his eye, approach
And speaking as an equal should,
Pick up some tricks from him...
If Ariel were bound again.

Ca(t)cophany

The grey cat cries
Outside the walls,
Prowls, with staring eyes,
Catches and mauls
A drifting moth—night denies
His wants, denial galls
The cat with yellow eyes
Who haunts the night and brawls
And cries, incessantly cries.

Cave-Dweller's Chant

The heavy-handed yellow wind
Flakes the river.
The thick reeds bend.
We flake wise-shaped flints
To hunt swift-hooved herds,
The rare red deer and reindeer,
The high-shouldered bison:
And in this dark deep place
Whose mouth defies the wind,
We make ourselves their images,
Their speed and their standstill
To keep in this close-mouthed place,
In this way to take the bison,
The reindeer and red deer,
To take their swiftness
And their stillness
Through our hands to command them
That the kill may be great
And great our feasting,
That we may dance, bending
As the reeds bend, full-bellied,
Sweating in the yellow wind.

Closed Loops

Cool sand at night
Shifts under-foot,
Drifts between the toes;
       Nearer to the water-line,
       Damp sand moulds
       Heel and arch and sole;
              And now the water swirls
              Around the feet and then
              Retreats; farther out,

A scattering of foam, waves
That curl and lightly crash
And, see, from the rim of the world,
       The moon has laid a path
       Across the water whose depths
       In silence breed such forms
              Of life as lurk behind
              The drifting doors of sleep—
              Hush, not tonight,

Please, for words may draw
Life from roiling depths,
Giving it aim and force,
       While words alone might not
       Dispel those lurking shapes—
       No, not tonight,
              For, see, the moon sets,
              The shimmering trail fades,
              And mere stars prevail.

II.

Boys and girls come down
To the beach at dusk, in twos
And threes, or one by one;
       Let tonight, each prays,
       Blaze with special stars
       For me—relentless, shrill,
              They wait: a Frisbee soars
              Out of reach; mist
              Rises; the waves recede.
Young faces, shrewd
Or sweet, seem incomplete,
Stare at the world, sulk—
       It takes years to compose
       A face, teach it to wear
       A pleased and pleasing look
              Teaching it to lie a bit
              For the sake of civility and pride
              Smoothing the ravages of what,
In disbelief and rage,
One had to learn—though some
Refuse, take pride in scars,
       Count rudeness, truth;
       And some, as if the world
       Would never see and read,
              As if they couldn't choose
              The stamp they'd wear, display
              The vacancy of their dismay.

III.

    The world is gaudy and round:

From over its wide rim

The perfumed stranger comes;

        Faces and hands flash

        In the sunlight; a lilting voice

        Shimmers in the dusk; each word,

                A spell; the harvest moon

                And evening star swell

                In the vast, promising sky—

Fool: the flashing hand

May wield a knife; words

May cut, leave aching scars:

        The dusty stranger comes

        To buy or sell; and the moon

        And stars blankly pull

                And get pulled, as the world,

                Incongruous, crooked, dull,

                Pulls and gets pulled—

Friends: what if the world

Is prismatic, colored and marked

By what each squinting eye

        Can see? When we are done,

        Let strangers from another sun

        Come, assess the world

                Our vision made, and tell

                The waiting galaxy of this,

                Our work of folly and rage.

Cogito Ergo Sum

Tentative
Shape without claims
Became aware of being
On the edge of a space
And about

To let go
As if there would unfold
Some means to hold its own
According to whatever might
Or might not

Be there
As if what was not known
Would of course be good
Would uphold, as if to be
Should mean

To go on
Being, grew aware of light
Lurking behind these dim
Fixed notions, saw through
Them, reeled

And reached
Inward, groping among them
For a sure hold, jarred loose
Parts, marred the design
Went on

To search
The dark shambles, to track
Obscure leads into tunnels
Blocked by rock falling
Suddenly

Drew back
Reminded of a blind impulse
Before, at an outer expanse
And caught between the two
Magnitudes

Discovered
Itself as what, perceiving
Both, heated in a friction
Of terrors, had to be
In between

To reach
In or out, make rules, set
Limits, give names, see
Designs, knew then it knew
And was.

Counter-Thrust

Never can human mind
All creation wholly conceive,
Nor for human being find
Wholesome reprieve:

Worlds without name,
Range without bound;
Dark matter, flame,
Silence and sound;

The nerves in throes;
The hand that tends,
Tearing what grows;
Words beyond amends.

Yet faith upholds
What even faith cannot define
And love in love beholds
Aspects of cosmic design.

Displacements

When we moved out of the waters,
　Drew ourselves out of the shallows
　　Onto the first rock-strewn beaches,
　　　And huddled in the morning winds
　　　　That diluted the stench
　　　　　Of slimy weeds and decaying crabs
　　　　　　And blew off the ravening flies,
　　　　　　　We were dazzled by the play of light
　　　　　　　　Through the thinner medium
　　　　　　　　And wondered at the hard outline
　　　　　　　Of each rock, each blade of swordgrass,
　　　　　　And the distant mountain ridge.

We also discovered the stark identities
　Of those we had known all our lives,
　　Even of those we had loved. Yet,
　　　We had no suspicion of how, after,
　　　　We would lose touch, no premonition
　　　　　Of how we would have to strain
　　　　　　To keep upright from then on,
　　　　　　　In the thin air that could not reconcile
　　　　　　　　The inconsistent motions of our bodies
　　　　　　　　With a sense of continuous purpose.
　　　　　　　Lost, the flow of limbs, lost
　　　　　　With the simple mind, the soft perception.

I can almost believe I was there myself,
  Shaking the water from briny, matted hair,
    Shivering a bit, too excited
      To be fully aware. Sometimes even now,
        When I look around, my breath catches—
          I am blinded by the intelligence
            Of sight. When I go back to the sea,
              Plunging into the great-bellied waves
              Or halting, ankle-deep, in the shallows,
                I feel the tug of ancient habits:
                  It is too late—perforce
                One recapitulates the ancestral choice.

And more, must have or make occasions
  To risk identity or prove that it resides
    In willing risk—so we, or our progeny,
      Will break from this refulgent earth,
        Escape its settled orbit and our star
          To range through universal space.
            What comforting unities we may lose,
              What compensating sense, may find,
                We cannot guess, and those who venture out
                  And come back and see through changed eyes
                Those who watched and only dreamed of going,
              May never find a way to let them know.

Yet—as if one has already suffered
  The stress of shifting gravities
   And the senses cramped within the frail,
    Safe-guarding shell, and the mind dilated
     Before the boundlessness beyond, as if
      One has already surveyed so many worlds,
       Such unhuman combinations of features
        That had to be reckoned as faces,
           Such ungodly notions of cause and consequence,
           Such unearthly tastes in cookery
          And copulation—that seemliness, even now,
         Requires many self-quelling silences.

Perhaps the nerve-ends are split
  Before the fact, in the act of imagining
   That compels the risk, enabling the fact:
    When the native tongue seems lovely,
     And arbitrary enough to be Sanskrit,
      And the birthplace, as much a myth as Troy
       Or Dome-City on Mars, and home means
        A walled space with no final coordinates,
         And one pauses daily upon awakening
          To recollect where one has got to, then
           For all one's commonplace talk and activity,
           One is drifting in fathomless oceans of space.

Elsinore

(New York City)

This city makes a monstrous Elsinore
That compounds
The thick and quick of men enmassed
And height and breadth of masonry
To breed more shapes
Than stars can be counted
In the small sky of its crowded night
Where murmurs of "Remember me..."
Perplex the unguarded ear.

Hamlet was informed,
Could point to culprits,
Name their crime, give it firm image
And fix his horror there—
Our ghost but lurks,
Does not declare himself,
And we attach to no single instance
Our trembling response that therefore invests
All the scene with dire fictions.

So we wonder what crucial thing
We've left undone that fills
The night with broken airs
Though no one's in the street but us
And these buildings give
No sign of tenancy save sleep.
Thus blind remorse

30

Makes strutters of us all and begs
Our questions by extravagance of speech.

Rhetoric articulates, yet also mocks
The heart that else would have us shouting
"Damn…" or leave us mute and laughterless;
But if Hamlet's each of us,
We're all of Elsinore as well:
Live and die by turns,
Betray, accuse, defend,
Play tricks upon ourselves
To find our madness out…

Yet, in the end, most of all, Horatio,
We stay to tell the wonders we have seen.

Epilogue

The old one sits,
Sightless, she sways and mumbles
Thanking God that she lives.

In a corner of her porch
A bit of sunshine falls.
There, she sits and, unseeing,
Knits with faded yarns
That she has often raveled
And rewound and knit again.

She says the hardships she
Has suffered were worse by far
Than her neighbor's, who is dying.

Spring sunshine feels good,
She says, and if her roof
Leaks in the rain, it is still
A roof, and, with her gnarled
Memories—she laughs
Quietly—all her own.

Esplanade #2

Come!—and we turned a corner
And found ourselves upon an esplanade...

It is winter; the face is stiff with cold
And the ears, filled with bitter wind.

> The chestnut vendor at the corner
> Shifts his cart to face the crowd;
> His eyes glitter; his breath,
> Congealing, wreathes his head;
> He stamps his feet for warmth
> And stirs his roasting nutmeats;
> Their fragrance fills the air.

January; the ornaments and snow are gone;
A sudden threat of spring is in the wind.

> The juggler in Parisian streets,
> He oils his body and the soot
> Catches in the folds of his flesh;
> He hefts a set of bolts and chains
> And squints to gauge his take;
> On Sunday he fishes in the Seine,
> Hatted, respectable, his cravat black.

Air from mouldy cellars merges with fog; the street,
A stage-set; voice and gesture over-project.

In Japan a woman is judged
By the back of the neck;
Though we make a moon of nacre
To crown the purple mountain,
We must also take unblemished plums
In silver tissue paper to soothe
The shifty, green-eyed gods.

April; rain all night; thunder; lightning;
At daybreak, the city is luminous and fresh.

The dolphin used to love us
When we were young and Greek
And, chanting at our oars, foundered
And, but for him, had drowned;
Kin to the almighty whale, he heaves
Himself above the waves to breathe
And seems ironically to smile.

The small hours of a stifling August night
And even near the river, there is no relief.

Once the forest here was thick;
Suppose the quick-eyed Indian
Stalking game, left behind his shadow,
Poised and ready for the kill;
Suppose that many years from now
Someone perceives the shape of our quest
And also feels it as a chill.

It is fall; the brilliant days grow short;
New construction juts toward the stars.

Gabriel, who gave the Word to Mary
And to Mohammed gave the Book, now stands
Upon a pseudo-gothic apse, commands
The University, the Presidential Tomb,
Convergences of traffic on the Drive,
Trumpet at his lips, he does not bend,
Cannot speak; his grace is iron-bound.

The winds shift and sweep away our words; debris
And dry leaves whirl at our feet; we drift apart.

Et Ego, Mr. Eliot?

I have turned as one turns
From importunate questioning;
I have turned.
I have turned
For a semblance of motion
And emotion
And from weariness with attitudes held
And upheld.
I have turned
Because turning is a negation
That implies affirmation.

Forgiven are the trespassers;
Forgiven are they;
Forgiven are the trespassers
For they come of a hungry land.

At the border of His dominion
I have placed a hitching post
And tethered there my mule.
There at the very border
I have placed my mark
And upon the clean sand
Where there is no sustenance.
And I shall return
When turning again from the multitude

To the seeking,
From the speaking
To the solitude.

For this is the kingdom;
For this is the kingdom of hayseed
And ragweed;
For this is the kingdom. Come.

In the courtroom
Is a gavel to pound.
I shall turn from the sound.
In the drawing room,
Plump pillows to hallow plump backs.
I shall turn.
In the parks of the city
Are hillocks and counterfeit mounds.
I shall return no more.

Our bread is dry;
Dry are the crusts and the cakes;
Our bread is dry:
It shall be given, eaten and given.

I shall be anthologized
And utilized
In the classroom I will be recited
And indicted
For my passion

And my dispassion,
For my assumptions
And my presumptions.

I shall not answer
Having turned from importunate questioning
Because turning is a negation
That implies affirmation.

Extractions

I.   Tides of the blood
     Flood the mind:
     Blind.

        Deep-sea swells
        Well in the flesh:
        Unbind.

           Fresh winds in play
           Fray the nerves:
           Remind.

     II.   Made of stone—
           And at the core
           Something stirred.

              Made of earth—
              And from the lump
              A cry half-heard.

                 Made of thought—
                 And in the body
                 Blurred.

III.   The old woman shrugs:

        A fragment falls from the sky,

        Hits a pond, hisses, and dies;

        A wisp of steam flits

        Across the saffron moon;

        The sleepers stir, but go on

        With their baffling dream.

Fulfillment Too Long Deferred...

Half a winter's snow was wanting
To transmute the bitter cold
And the stark outlines of the city,
But when, at last, it fell,
Fulfillment too long deferred,
It fell as reflection upon the eye,
Out of touch with the moment,
And the pulse failed to quicken.

It was like an incident, faded,
But for lack of new ventures,
Recorded in a journal before daybreak,
In those flat hours when landmarks
And street signs are lost in a blur
Of weariness, smoke, fog
Or some other soft estrangement,
In words that seem cold and dim—
For there is nothing to add to a scene
When the play of feeling is gone
And the figures are oversimplified
By time—but, then, timeless sorrows
Drift into mind, stopping
The channels of useful enterprise,
Like thickly falling snow.

The Hedge

On the other side of the hedge
They speak of a game lost
By a technical error. Red hair
In sunlight, copper, bare skin, bronze.
They laugh. Birds chirp.
Ice clinks in someone's glass.

On this side of the hedge
An empty chair rocks in the wind.

On the other side of the hedge,
This morning, three children:
You must be superman, says one;
I want to be a shark, says two;
You must be the daddy, says three.
They giggle and agree to play house.

Tonight, moonlight dapples a crowd;
A guitar, laughter, songs. At dawn,
A few still linger and talk.

On this side of the hedge
Shadows suggest the grotesque
And yet, I would not choose
To go round to the other side—
I might lose a double advantage.

Hour of the Sybil

Silence, sifting down like thick snow,
Filters a pale, even light
Through the darkness;
Voices, visions, drifting
Through the solitude,
Fall into place
And show their compelling design;
Eyes that used to cling
To the rich color and rare form
In common things,
Now see only what they mean
And the ear is filled with their harmony.
How still, the hands and feet;
Even the blood seems spellbound;
I am a stone set in a whirlwind.

I do not know how long this hour lasts,
But day must break
Into its too perfect sphere.

Interregnum #1

Although faith be whole,
Grief intrudes
Turning the subject soul
From ordered certitudes
To lawless yearning.

Although faith molds
The function it exacts
To the scheme that enacts
It, as armature, holds
The flesh upright,

Grief, by self-denial fused,
Denies the use of self,
Will stifle, keep faith blind,
Bind hands and feet,
Make stumble and weep.

Though the soul be staked
On death's acquittal
Of its riddled case,
To endure the interval,
It surmises, sues for Grace.

Interregnum #2

When shifting tensions strike
A momentary balance, then
Suddenly time falls away;
Air turns soft and luminous;
Words submerge in what they name;
Flesh, substantial now as mind,
Works as blithely as it plays;
Fresh and fair, like Grace, perhaps:
Motionless in graphic flux,
Vivid, strict, and heedless, this
Paradox more bright than sleep
Binds itself to free itself,
Casts no shadow, knows no shame;
Fullness of the sea and earth
Enters into blood and bone;
Quick of moment moves the mind
In ornate continuum
Its essential route to find…
But Grace is known when Grace is gone:
The striking hours impose again:
Tides of urgency and enigmatic winds
Sweep in, trammel up the registry of fact,
And make the actor doubt his fairest act.

Interregnum #3

The derivation of an act
Or moment acted in,
Its perfect revelation
Would dissolve event and hour
And whoever witnessed it;

To square a given time,
So it seems absolved in deed,
Debit freed, its harmony
Apparently resolved,
Does not dispose of it;

It earns no graceful pause,
Awards no pristine starting place;
As cause in disparate effects,
Distracting permutations
Are imposed by it;

No formulation of the vast
Continuum is more
Than tentative: what man's
Redemptive will and work—
At truest pitch—construe of it;

This vocation makes us plunge,
Keep pace within the flux—
Yet, so prismatic, so proof it is,
That, with illumination or
Without, we are resolved in it.

Interval

I.

The lady in the kitchen,
Scoring half a ham, draws her knife
Through the smooth white fat, criss, cross:
Voices in her mind, meanwhile, spatter
Against her inner ear

> So I told him I
>
> Would not   He said
>
> He was busy   She swore
>
> She had tried   They
>
> Did not understand

She stoops to light the oven, then begins
To stud the ham with cloves

> No openings   I cannot
>
> Afford to   You're
>
> Stupid

> She bastes the ham

With cider, pats brown sugar on, pours
Some cider in the pan, opens the oven door,
Sets the ham within, shuts the door

> But why   Then how
>
> Not even if

The table set, the wine cold, dinner
Can be served in an hour and a half; nothing left
To do but wash her hands, touch her wrists
And earlobes with scent, wait for the guests to arrive.

II.

                     She stands at the window
Withdrawing from the household behind her;
The trees that line the street below
Are lashed by wind and rain, rain
That sheets against the window panes;
Lightning splinters the sky, burns off
The images left over from the kitchen work;
Thunder crashes, strikes from her mind
The small sharp voices, their patterns
Of woe, their familiar intrusions; she rests
                In her own stillness.
Then, the clouds thin and scatter
And sunlight splashes her, standing there
At the window, waiting for the doorbell to ring
                As a child, in the house
Alone, late one afternoon, she had played
At the window sill with a prism, turned it
In the slanting light, caught a rainbow,
Splashed it on her hand, spilled it on the floor
                        They've forgotten
                        Don't care   Won't come
        She closes her eyes,
From this darkness of her own devising
To slip into the passages of time, to find
Again the doorways of houses that once
Were home or where she came to visit,
And the faces, dimly smiling or mouthing
Words she cannot hear, the faces

49

Of those whose paths have diverged from hers
                    Who went away
                    Who stayed behind
                    Who cut short their lives
Other faces that she has since seen
Clarified or blurred by the stresses of time,
And one, the half strange face
Of a child hinting somewhat at the image
Of an old woman, or an old face
Modeled over that of a child, that face, her own.

III.

                    She opens her eyes,
Emerges into the light, still at the window;
The old woman implicit, dallies with oblivion,
Rehearsing a universe where she will not be,
And discounts the transitory
                    They will come   but
                    What use their coming
                    What use the breaking
                    Of bread   the breaking
                    Of silence
            Meanwhile, laughing,
And her laughter laps at far away shores,
Eddies around unknown planets, ripples
Out to the stars.   The child, ignored,
Retreats to a long abandoned realm

And they came to her

And she served them

Out of a golden cup

And yet the cup was full

And the bright smell of the food and its taste

And how she moved, bearing the cup,

Gravely smiling, full of grace

They said she was good

They wanted to come again

They wanted to stay

And the child drifted

Until her voice was lost. The old woman shrugged

Knowing well that realm

And the frail wall around it, long ago

Laid waste and yet implicit

In the walls of a household, in the stocked shelves

Of a pantry, in the rows of books and the etchings

Of sunless landscapes and architectures haunted

By still, small figures, implicit

In the kept order of a household but also

In the effort to gauge oblivion before the walls

Of the flesh break down and the self scatters

Witless in the dust; the old woman retires,

Holding on to her mind so as not to fall

Before her time into time out of mind.

IV.

The woman at the window

Turns away, moves to the center of the room

Whose ordered space agrees with her sense

Of order and space, meets her craving

For stillness, and wherever she stands, however moves,

She makes no stir in this room;

She feels the propriety of such accord; it is sweet;

She savors it; also tastes its bitterness, feels

Its impropriety, even its peril

But those who come to visit

Will break up the stillness, shape, accord,

And the room will eddy with their voices and hers

The weather   The traffic

This administration   Our son

Your mother   My dentist

Tell him he's wrong

They are always the same,

However different. Then she will ask them to table;

She will carve and serve, pour the wine.   Later,

When she is all by herself, with the voices in her mind,

Then, she will rehearse, explain, resist, resolve

What do you know about politics

What do you know about people

This looks good   I have ideals

Don't be naïve   I'm hungry

The truth   Pass the salt

You're joking   Each to his taste
        People are impossible   We are people
At last the doorbell rings. She starts. And now,
She smells the baking ham. The smell is good.
Gladly she goes to welcome in the guests.

In the Sea, a Stone

In the motley sea a white stone,
Ground round by the laughter
Of numberless grains of sand,
By winding currents
Moved to an end no words set:
Let that stone, fine in proportion
As to the naked eye it seems,
Be lodged, though amid debris,
Upon the ocean floor
Whose depth shall not be sounded
Where even brightest sunlight
Cannot reach, save perhaps,
As a solitary golden mote;
And I'll speak for this as token
Of my measurable love, saying:
Here is the contour of my heart;
Weigh it, try it—and if it shatter
I shall insist, laughing,
It was only a token,
And toss the fragments back into the sea.

Often I linger at the tideline
Licking the salty spray from my cheeks.

Letter from Kyoto

Water runs busily in the deep gutters
Along Kyoto streets. In Moenjodaro,
Too, drains were carefully laid out,
Covered here and there by stone slabs;
But no water runs in them—Moenjodaro
Has been dead some four thousand years.

Seventeen hundred temples and shrines,
Imperial palaces of a thousand years—
Handsome roofs behind long, high walls:
Wherever gates open, tourists enter;
Sight-seeing seems to have displaced
Excessive piety and protocol in Kyoto.

Beyond the garden and huddled roofs,
A low wall of hills: myriads of green
That quicken or fade as the clouds
Lift, thicken, shift—I could remain
At the window of my room in Sukyo-Ku,
Kyoto, all day long and for many days.

I wander through Kyoto, map in hand—
Signs also indicate the famous gardens;
I prefer the Imadegawa Street bridge
Where, the Takano having joined
The Kamo River, the rapidly flowing water
Shows a persistent reddish stain.

Lullaby

Wait a while, a year, a day—
This sorrow shall pass away:
     As sunlight into dusk
     And leaves into coal
     And a lovely voice
          Into silence.

Wait a while, a day, a year—
The pain shall disappear:
     As shores under sea
     And coals under flame
     And a costly silence
          Under song.

Wait a while, a year, a day—
This life shall pass away:
     As cosmos into void
     And flame into smoke
     And a shapely song
          Into thin air.

Meditation at a Window

Perhaps to the Old-Timers
(As to the Greeks in particular
Many colors were more or less purple)
Several kinds of fruit
Were more or less apples.

This hypothesis occurs to me
As I sit at the window on a quiet night,
Looking out beyond the rowhouses
And the moon emerges
Momentarily from the clouds.
The scene is traditional;
It is nonetheless effective.

Troy in the mind renews her doom;
Her walls in flame, fall.
The changes have been rung
The world around: armaments vary
But the essential downfall recurs.
This scene is also traditional,
Is also still effective
So that we are minutely scarred
By a perpetual disaster
That is our own disaster
Where— and whenever it strikes,
Or by our sense of its perpetual imminence.

An apple (glossy and firm,
No worm-speck upon it)
As the very Form of the Indigestible,
The occasion of public discord
And calamitous strife, of disobedience
And a more primitive, ineluctable fall.

(Newton, an exception,
Whose falling apple evoked no more
Than its own immediacy, no hint
Of tragic flaw, merely an instance
Of physical law, merely gravity.)

The apple, then, as instigation
Of this era and of its nightmares
That course the sleep of generations
Who stumble again from the simple garden;
Or grope in dark winds for the first home,
A hometown all Troy to an infant's eye,
That had seemed the fulcrum of the world;
Or hurtle, screaming struck dumb,
From cliff and tower and rooftop.

(Another exception, the sleep-walker
Who stepped from his window,
Fell three stories,
Somersaulting twice in air,
Landed on his feet, knees flexing,
And walked, naked, down the street.)

Rare is the man who may dream
Of an apple as a thing in itself.
The insidious worm may do so;
As a bird, roosting for the night
Upon a high branch, may dream
Of a long, winding worm;
Or a cat on a cushion, of a bird;
Or a particular, a rather dimpled lady,
Buying butter and cream at the corner store,
May dream of a cat curled in her lap,
A Persian, even a blue cat;
And the bland clerk behind the counter
May dream of the lady partly stripped,
Caught in the act of stripping...

I postulate a world webbed in dreams,
Itself dreaming and dreamt of—why not?
Yet, sitting at the window,
Aware of the unregarding street
That sleeps and stirs
Beneath the pinkish overcast,
I am wary of such things, dreams
And speculations about dreams.

Memorandum

Let me defend myself against the sea:
Wading in, however sure I may be
Of the underlying grade, let me feel my way,
      Wary of sudden depths,
And of mindless, clawing things that lurk
On the bottom; let me heed the turn of a tide,
The sweep of a current, the breaking wave,
      And resist the enticing sea.

Let me mark a changing wind and clear
Sea-wrack from the beach; let me look
To the sea-walls, but also take note
Of shifts in sea lanes, keeping a way
      Through to this solitary isle,
Despite moonless nights and mists,
Storms or swells, or even the lull
      Of the all-consuming sea.

Neiges d'Antan

Down the snowbank we swept,
Three small children
Dovetailed on one small sled,
And at the bottom we spilled ourselves
Into the deep bed of snow
And laughed and laughed
Until Jane who had red hair
Made wet and went home.
I never saw her again,
Nor Barbara who was blonde and left
When the winter sun began to set.
I remember the bright faces
Flattened and framed
By bonnets and scarves,
And the postures we invented
To prolong our hilarity,
And how I pretended to steer
With my half-numbed feet
Though I knew it was the cant
Of the hill and its hummocks
Sped and lurched us on our way.
But before evening fell
When I had the sled to myself
(It was called the Snow King),
I rode on my belly and steered

With such sure hands
And shifting of weight,
I made it partway up the opposing slope.

You, too, Father, played in the snow
That Sunday afternoon,
Yet you never saw how, at first,
With all the bold children
On the hilltop showing off
Their skill, I quailed
And could not meet the momentum
Head on, nor how I clowned instead
Until, at last, as the light failed
Perforce, I took the flying start
And the long, fast curve of the course.
Now, though your height and dark hair
Must have shown in that white scene,
And I know the sled you took
Was called the Lightning Glider,
I have no sense of your presence there.

It was the summer after
And on a far-away shore that I found
Stretches of dunes and wanted to roll
Down the warm, shifting slopes—
But there were patches of sword-grass
Everywhere, and stranded
At the tide-line nearby, Medusas,
Great jellyfish with mottled hearts.

Daily we walked on the firm sand
Along the water's edge
And I skirted the quivering monsters
And averted my eyes, not that I expected
To be turned to stone if I stared,
But the name was ominous.
At last I came alone and dared myself
To look, even threw broken shells
At the largest Medusa of all:
Nothing happened, but my stomach knotted up
For I knew the creature was dying.
I think I sent you a postcard,
Father, that same afternoon,
Wishing you were there.

At sixteen, I went away to college.
It was my first winter in New England:
By December the pond was iced-over
And the river, frozen along its banks;
The rolling grounds
Were covered with snow so thick
It lasted till the end of February.
You were overseas; the war went on and on
And I wrote to you once a week
About my studies and dormitory life
And, always, the wonderful landscape,
Hoping thus to give proof
Of seriousness, a sense of humor
And many appreciations.

Yet I used to trudge in the snow for hours
Composing letters I could never send,
Letters, as to a friend,
Proving nothing, save, perhaps,
A loneliness equal to your own

Father, there has always been
Some sort of continent between us;
Tomorrow, when I write to you,
I shall not bring up
These ancient, irrevocable things
But I will mention
The thickly falling snow
That drifts voluptuously
Even in the streets of the city
And confirms an essential solitude
Equal to an essential community.

Nous Sommes Las*

We saw a man going toward a mine
And all he had with him
Was a small torch in his hand,
So we called to him—

        Danger ahead.

        Haven't you read the signs?

The man turned and looked our way
But said nothing
And we did not know if he saw us
Or heard what we had to say—

        The mine is deep,

        The passages wind;

        The shorings are rotten

        And your torch is small.

        What if the battery dies?

        What if the shorings fall?

And the man stood there
And stared and did not speak.

        The passages are steep,

        The footing, bad;

        At the bottom of the shaft

        The water is deep.

        Men go into that mine

        And never come out again.

* "We are weary" – Slogan of a French peasant rebellion, said to
have taken place in the reign of Henry of Navarre.

Still he waited and said nothing,
So we asked him—

        Why?

And then he did reply—

        Because I am tired
        Of night after day
        And day after night,
        The glaring sunlight
        And the shock of looking up
        And seeing stars.
        Because I am tired.
        I sleep through my dreams
        And cannot recall them
        And all morning long
        A shadow follows me
        That I follow all afternoon,
        And yet I cannot stand
        That moment when,
        The sun at its height,
        There is no shadow
        And no shade. I am tired.

We had, each of us, been there
Ourselves, so we gave him a nod
And let him go on to the mine
And we watched till it swallowed him up
And the small light of his torch.

Yes, we had been there
And, somehow, found a way out.

Whatever it was we had proved, now
We stood at the foot of a mountain
And each of us would have to climb
Although the signs read, Danger Ahead.

Paean

(New York City)

Green-bent, a wind
Stirs the swarthy air;
A river arteries
The simple flesh,
Frees the blood
To course the palisades
Or join the river's flux;
Hands touch at bridge-span;
Stone by air or water
Comes alive—Lord
The world's in my eyes.

Flesh is light
In wind's poise,
In agile silence cleaves
Resounding streets;
Wonder is the eye
Where, through debris,
Form made friend in form;
Blocks came together
And the City rose
At three rivers' beckoning—
Lord I am beholden.

Parallelogram

Beauty is not for the taking
And sometimes it lags:
 Intimation that stalls
 Until beauty grows cold;
And sometimes it leaps,
Illumination:
 Then it blinds;
But beauty's instilled
 Though it's not for the taking
When forms in mind and matter relate
And the senses quicken
And nothing daunts:
 Then beauty is all
 And in its dominion
 Obliterates transience.

Love is not to be looked for
And sometimes it goes begging:
 Temptation that palls
 Until love loses hold;
And sometimes it keeps
In limitation;
 Then it binds;
But love is fulfilled
 Though it's not to be looked for
When stone in hand and star equate
And the nerves are quenched

69

And nothing wants:

> Then love is whole
> And in its dominion
> Annihilates distance.

If time were lost in beauty
And space were lost in love,
The world would be undone:

> But joy needs no occasion,
> Heeds neither question nor cost,
> Nor is the world an evasion-

Though love is not to be looked for
And beauty is not for the taking.

Perspectives

In this mosaic
Of incalculable dimensions,
Luminous and interchanging,

That by order
And integration of its parts
Seems to transcend their sum,

So that death
Is merely a reversion of parts,
The release of borrowed breath,

And bulk self,
Merely the means to identify
And enact a temporary locality—

Yet in bulk self
If love discover a terminus
And limn its definitive shape,

Then mutability
And transcendent perspectives
Become a glaring impertinence.

Peter Milton's Studio

1. A patch of maple trees,
    Here and there, a birch;
    A stretch of clearing; beyond,
    The shallow, stony stream.
    The boy with a length of rope
    Dangling from his hand, stands,
    Watches the man with the pipe
    Coming across the footbridge.

        Behind the boy, grazing
        In the shade, a winged horse.

    A clearing in the tangle
    Of scrub; insects humming.
    The small girl holds a net
    Flush to a rock, regards
    The captured butterfly;
    The man leaning against the oak
    Regards the child;
    Smoke curls from his pipe.

        Behind the tree, grazing
        In the shade, a winged horse.

    A field; treefrogs chirp

And crickets; sporadic barking
Breaches the cold wall of night
And the stars are very sharp.
The man rests against the fence,
Smells the changing season—
Green going up in the cool flames,
Leaves falling and, soon, the snow.

Limned against the moonlight,
Briefly, the winged horse.

2.   I took the straight lines
My father conceived
And bent them to my need,
Telling myself, in these toils
Flight might be taken, tamed
And aimed at stars; in this maze,
Words be made to reveal
Their several sides
As they edge into silence;
In this intricacy be shown,
Unashamed, the arthritic roots
Of our rosiest, sweetest-smelling,
Richest blossomings.

I took the simple horizon
My father insisted on,

Broke it into segments useful

In a shifting landscape,

Telling myself, so bridges

Might be built to let us cross

The sudden chasms if we choose;

Lattices be devised

To brace the slipping hills;

And curving perpendiculars be

Set up to ground our vision,

Let it rise to measured heights

And then, hold, there.

My father's eyes and mine

Have met across the tilting fields.

3. Now a hollow barking pounds

The steep walls of night

And wakens bestial creeping humors

That claw the finespun mesh

Binding our vital processes,

And start chronic tremors in the spine.

Measure in the universe, too,

Is kept by pulsing networks

And were the stars unleashed

Their orbits snarled, they'd clash,

Fall in flames and planets, peoples,
Their acts of pride— all, lost.

What good then, wearing a hard hat
Tied down well over the ears,
Bathing in still waters only,
Burrowing into caves? Where hide
When earth quakes and sky falls?
How shut out broken, inner crying?

But come: see how these compliant stars
Make their rounds tonight—
And might we not, then, at last lie down,
Put off our haunted dreams

And sleep.

4.   We breakfasted together on Sunday
And over the sausages and eggs,
The honey and home-made bread,
We heard a broadcast
Of Landowska playing Bach.
Clear autumn light blended in
At the windows and for a moment
A humming-bird hovered in view.
Then it was time to go. I got up

And shook hands, saying, thank you,
It was lovely. Goodbye. Goodbye.

When I was well out of sight,
I left the winding road,
Passed through a copse
(Maple, here and there, a birch)
Into a field I had marked before:
A horse watches from the far end,
His wings, so neatly folded
White on white, might not even exist.
He tosses his head and snorts.
Across the vast and pitted field
         I make my way.

Pilgrim's Gambit

Let me stay by the river a while
To compose myself and take
My bearings, for when the sun
At meridian strips the landscape
It is not the place that seems
Strange, but my being there.

        Briefly   a cloud   blots out
        The sun   the river   darkens.

Let me be nameless on the edge
Of a crowd, abstaining from speech
Though words flow through my mind,
Unless winds blow in from the sea
Sweeping thoughts into a torrent
That amounts to stillness.

        Cloud masses shift weeds rustle
        And mice   scurry   out of sight.

Let those who have ties of place
Count on welcome and farewell
For, claimless, I am not moved
By profit or loss though, looking on,
I may pause as if stirred by old
Memories or long-forgotten hopes.

        A wind riles the river
        Hush and then cloudburst.

Plenum

*"And there is no object so soft but it makes
a hub for the wheeled universe."* Whitman

No small thing so soft and white,
So flickering, it may not confront,
Fill and focus sight;

And no thing so large, black and blunt,
It may not in the palm of the hand
Be formed and weighed;

And each known thing, bright or bland,
Has to be proved again and played,
Each time, redefined.

The very air is full of clinging shapes,
The eyes with them perforce aligned;
No hand escapes;

And no instant so sovereign, so free,
It does not conform with all time,
Bound in what may be;

And from the everlasting pantomime,
A sense of loss, a burden of demands—
Yet closed eyes contemplate

Enclosed perplexity and clenched hands
Reform no jot, not a line of the fate
The palms are said to anticipate.

Post-Mortem

The man with green and golden eyes
Remembering how he used to translate
Into elegant ratios his farthest sight,
So strict and clear he was, insists
It's not the inverted focus of his gaze
Distorts the light, makes him fumble,
But a kind of fog that gathers round
His head and clings—how and when
It began, well, he sighs, sinks back,
Folds his hands, lets his thought escape...

He starts again: sundown may splash flame
Between night and day, but cool flame
That cannot consume the miasma of day,
Cannot purge the tumults that break
Into night with monstrous dreams—
Besides, the sky is bland, our eyes
Endow the sky with that splendor
Which, having neither substance nor aim
May appeal to those whose need is blind
But is impertinent to a balanced mind...

His words, lingering in the dead air,
Lend bulk to his perplexity—he says
He thought his vantage point secure,
So ideal and unencumbered a space

It was, where he planned to strip
With adroit and antiseptic fingers
From the essential truth (divined
As diagram) its phenomenal sheath—
Admitting he felt a chill, he asserts
It was elation and proper to his case...

Then, in the thin unshielding air,
Truth unsheathed, dissolved—his stand
Shaken, he fell of his own weight:
Confessing that now he bates his breath
And waits for revelation, the man
With green and golden eyes, overcome
By rage, cannot enact his over-wrought
Conceptions; eyelids lowered, lips
Moving, he counts his pulse and falls,
Almost, into an attitude of prayer.

Preliminary Digression

I rehearse finalities, she said,
And how they may be shaped
From beginnings, forced at turning points,
Until they cannot be escaped.

These predictions, she shook her head,
'Projections' is more precise,
Do not always come to pass—the joints
Made in the mind are too nice

To match the larger, looser departures
Of reality from an apparent line
Or its unexpected continuities,
And yet I am impelled to define

And suffer in advance such failures
As culminate in the shutting of a door,
The perfection of all one's anxieties
In a half-death one has always known before.

So I study every confrontation coming,
Its corners and cut-offs, where they can be,
The irrevocable word, how it blinds,
Express, explore my own inadequacy

Until, at last, the jars numbing
One's nerves into acquiescence,

In the prospect of finality one finds
Ironic propriety, desperate recompense.

I am not simple, she said, cannot deride
The gods or men or institutions
If my investments do not grow,
Nor blame myself for dark suspicions.

She shrugged. I distrusted pride,
Despised bargaining, could not bend,
Would not mock beauty nor set faith low—
My chosen means wind me to a choiceless end.

But come, let's talk of other things
And make the most of what this hour brings.

Prologue

The child in the corner
Hides a half-smile
And the pains he takes
With the images he makes
Of his triumphs tomorrow.

He turns back his tears
To feed a secret fountain;
The basin fills,
The stream gushes out:
Surely the child will not drown,
Will know to drift
With the greater current,
Will surely seize the tide,
Though the stream should swell
Till the world is swept
By swift waters.

In a corner, a child
Hides a half-smile.

Salaam Aleikoom

For Rifat Jehan Rashid

On a hot April afternoon
In the Shalimar Gardens,
We sat down together
On the sparse grass and
Brushing off persistent flies,
Talked through the nine years
Since we used to sit and talk
Near the Hudson River:
In time's durance we had grown
So strictly like ourselves,
We could recognize each other
And speak immediately
As old friends who live
Half a world apart must speak,
Under the wing of death
And other implacable distances.

Later, I showed you how to blow on grass
And the noise made you laugh and laugh.

Scope

Hail, splattering
The swollen river;

Heavy, stippled river
Pouring into the sea;

Backwash, churning;
Beyond, the sea merging

With the grey, spitting sky;
Grey sea and sky

Closing in on the mind
And the swollen, churning

Splattered mind, opening,
Holds sky, sea, river, hail.

Seascape with Figures

Between a heavy, yellow sea
And a long, low cliff of grey rock
Tufted with stiff grass
And crowned with scrub,
Spreads a strip of coarse, clean sand;
Into the overcast, some brightness
Is diffused from behind the cliff;
There's wind—the grasses bend
And the waves are foam-flecked.

The man at the water's edge
Plays a taut line: his rod arches
With the weight of his catch
And his back and shoulders act
As a tighter, buttressing arch;
Clothed in dim tones of brown,
Wearing a cap, his face unseen,
He is intent upon his sport
And has become his action.

Nearer, a boy lies on his belly,
Waves bare feet idly in the air,
Chin in hand, stares out to sea;
His profile is still unformed;
Wind plays with his hair,
Sand gathers in the folds

Of his dungarees and denim shirt;
Heedless, even of the fish in play,
He is wrapt in, he is his dream.

In the foreground, a woman sits;
Arms resting on the arms of her chair;
Brown hair in heavy coils;
White stole swathing her throat,
Shoulders and breast; face, exposed
And her all-and-nothing seeing stare;
The man left his creel, the boy,
His sneakers in her keeping; her back
To them, it is of them she is aware.

In the woman's figure, the man's and boy's
Compose: the tensions unresolved in one,
The unfinished features of the other
Meet in her elemental pose—
Settlement of chair and limbs, folds of cloth,
Inward-looking eyes, density, stillness;
She serves as foil to the span of sky
And ragged stretch of cliff; her weight
Seems equal to the weight of the sea.

Set-Piece

The titmouse cried twice
From the holly bush, a branch
With fading berries fell
Into a pool of mud, the owl
Flew across the highway—

                      shadow
Against moonlight, splash
In shallow water, tremor of leaves.

The fat woman in the armchair
Heaved with silent laughter
Till the tears streamed
From her eyes and she was blinded
And could not hear—

                      then the knife
Struck and the world stopped
Between two heartbeats.

When the red mist had lifted
And the sky turned out to be blue
With a few clouds that shifted
From one mild shape to another—
Nothing to gape at;
When the sun rose and set
As it always had, three days running,
And the stars, too, even Hesperus,

According to the season;
When several women gave birth
With no more pain and blood than usual
To wholesome boys and girls,
The people went back to business
And the older children,
To their lessons and sports.

Yet such a tale of murder
And the return of ghosts
And other dark cravings,
Is told many times
At the long tables of scrubbed white pine
And the round tables of waxed oak
As the sunlight pales
And, later, before the fire
Over ale or mulled wine and hazelnuts.
But when the wind
Blows cinders and smoke
Back into the room, the people move away
Shielding their faces, losing their thread;
Then the spell breaks
And they cannot meet each other's eyes.

As the knife drove home
It set my teeth on edge.

I did not think of my death
But of how I had let it happen
Knowing the attempt would be made,
Knowing the soreness of the heart,
The blank in the mind, the hot, wet hand,
The darkened blade—

                For survival

Insight is not enough.

Soliloquy

My name is David.
I have not yet come to grips
With Goliath, but the veins
In my right hand stand out
And my shoulder already aches.

I remember that in early morning
I used to leap surely from stone to stone
Instead of taking a straight path.
Even then I frowned, and when I stumbled
My hands grew cold and my cheeks burned.

From where I stand now
I seem to see to the rim of the world.
I sometimes think it's not so very large:
It fits within my eye
Or the swing of my arm.

But in the evening I go down
Where my kinfolk are,
For I am called David
And it was also written that I
Should play a lyre and sing.

A Song and a Dance

She stands still and laughs,
Letting the sun go down, runs,
Going nowhere, leaps from rock
To rock where the sea churns,
And, laughing, lets the sun rise.

Air is her Sunday garment,
Shining, warm, seamless,
It cannot be bought by the yard,
Rain does not make its colors bleed
Nor its subtle fibres shrink.

But, a hawker of seashells,
She does, for the marketplace,
Put on a more compliant look
That may be fingered
And appraised while she calls:

> Seashells for sale—faultless
> Their whorls and pink luster. Sir,
> Here's the real thing—I took it
> Fresh from the sea yesterday.
> Lady, it is clean.

93

Sonnet

As you and I from different courses drew
A common source of strength, an ancient code,
And in the quaintest visions each one knew
The other recognized his normal mode,

We might have cleared a broadly speaking road
Through this dumbfounded world and noisy age
And eased each other's solitary load
Of splendid useless words and stifled rage

Or made of our bare and darkened stage
A very tempest's eye of sacred rest
In which whole-hearted friends alone engage
Who know and therefore trust each other best;

But your defection now, makes me defy,
Unmanned, the vulgar blast, the blackened sky.

Squall

Central Park, an island set
In traffic and seas of noise—yet
Here are open skies and trees
In fresh leaf, grass newly mown,
Winding paths, April airs;
On the pond, model ships, blown
By a fitful breeze, roll, tack,
At last, sail safely back;
Here at noon Miranda comes
To stroll; the Ferdinand she needs
Does not appear; her hour gone,
She wonders if he was left behind
Upon a distant shore or drowned
Or so changed, he wears the shape
Of Caliban; alone at night she weeps—
And there is no Prospero to spell from air
The symmetrical response to a maiden's prayer.

Susannah Among the Ruins

She had no experience of war
And bombs had never fallen on her city,
But when planes passed low over Manhattan
She would see the skyscrapers waver,
Then, crumple into each other,
And the rock-based island seemed to shake…

The dust and the silence settled
Over the vast heaps of rubble;
A few walls stood
And some corroded steel frameworks
Jutted into the sky, their angles,
Wrong; she could see clear across
From the East River to the Hudson…

She watched a lean cat
Stalking its own illusions
Or a flock of pigeons nibbling
At loose dirt and bits of brick
In the bright spring sunlight
Where fractured bones cast
Mastodon shadows and weeds

Were thick, already flowering,
Blue, yellow, white…

And why should she linger there,
Like one of the stubborn dead,
Hovering over the broken monster,
Deaf, mute, futile…

But the vision would last only a moment,
Pass with the low-flying planes
And leaves no mark on the world
Or on the part she played, for she
Had no experience of war
And no bombs had fallen on her city.

Theme and Variations

I.

At last, darkness
And the universe expands.

I cannot expound galactic motion
In space that is finite but boundless,
Nor the perpetual eastern rising of the sun ,
No, nor the Hudson River that flows
Always within the margin of its shores—
I come to the verge of a comprehensive statement
And then gross mortality, overcharging the humanistic eye,
Refutes the perfect river, the obliging star, the definitive cosmos.

Sometimes a belly-full of laughter interferes.
I have no theory for this.

II.

I'll put it another way:
It is day and the universe contracts.

This summer morning there's a wind full of fresh sea-air,
And fine light brushes the Hudson, the Palisades
And all the brute geometry of our streets
Into the semblance of a pure and simple world—

But the grocery clerk down the block
Who paints in oils, prefers abstractions,
Says every man has to express himself
And it's not the object
But the nourishment it gives the eye.
Take this peach, he says; holds it up at arm's length;
Squints at it. See what I mean? Or take that peach
There, he says; points to a shapely customer in shorts.
No, he says, I'll take that one. He laughs.
Several ladies laugh too.

And there's the daily round—thought
Fixed in the shape of habitual need:
The struggle for footing
Exhausts the desire to explore;
Routine eases distress and dulls
The response to sudden loveliness.

And consider the hierarchies, commercial and industrial,
Financial, political, theological; the competition
Of the arts, the professions, the sciences, social and physical;
And the needs of the aged and the infantile,
The ill-adapted and the overly-adapted,
The crippled man, the colored man, the foreigner,
The common man and the uncommon man.

The jargons of polite intelligence
Indicate but cannot express this;
They have a cautious strict propriety.

The language of jazz expresses
But cannot resolve this;
It too has a propriety.
While the ceaseless jawing in the street
That gives makeshift satisfaction to raucous appetites,
Has neither shape nor wit to encompass this.

But then, when dusk comes,
People leaning from their windows
Stare mildly at familiar streets
Or sit talking on the stoop,
And there's a stillness about them:
Perhaps submission to fatigue,
Or an effect of half-light and humidity,
Or a premonition of relief,
A luminous dream that is really always there.

What's to be made of all this,
Can it be graphed—time coordinate with space,
Tracing a straight foreseeable line—
Or is there something more to it
Than meets the eye?

III.
At nightfall the eye can be exercised
As far as the smallest pinpoint star.

Shadow enlarges on the stated contours of our world
And no limit is set upon conception.

Think now of that measurable space without bounds,
And how the universe will end:
Golden whirling galaxies,
Like human things, gone to dust.

God, what a stillness then.
But we that have fore-witnessed the dread fact
Must not linger there: absolute silence
 Shatters the eardrum, blinds
And breaks the inner organs and the will.

Besides, another era surely will propose
Some other cosmic image. The truth
Is neither here nor there and for the sake
Of our health, mental and physical,
And our activities, social and political, and
As it has been said, for the sake of the love
We bear our elders, our progeny and peers,
We will not enter into the realm of metaphysics;
We will abstain from those questions that have no answers.

This is a bargain most of us have made
And broken, remake and break again.
Take the grocery clerk who paints:

He says his present phase is metaphysical;
It will not last; he says so himself.

I knew one man refused to back down,
Said the only questions leading anywhere
Were those without answers,
And that the world of our striving and sense-perceiving
Crudely diagrammed the life that moved beneath-beyond it all;
Said even the apparent stars pointed elsewhere
And in time astronomers would learn to read;
Said certain drugs could free the potent inner eye
And he had seen the sun and moon cross the sky and dance,
And all the graphic everlasting souls of things.
This, though not the proof he sought, was reassuring
And he seems to thrive now, who used to cry for love of God
That loved not him and would not speak.

Strange, isn't it, what becomes of old friendships:
With the discovery that all's been said and done
They pass into memory and are justified.

IV.
Said mediocre in the ranks of the stars,
Our sun, procreant, ravager and benefactor,
Unmoved by the idolatry of a thousand generations
Or by our pragmatic speculations,
Still compels our servitude and spurs

Our will to find in heaven and on earth
A purpose mindful of our destiny.

The fellow who works in the grocery
Tells me how he used to hate it there
Day after day and having to paint at night—
What the electric light did to his colors
Was enough to make him sweat—but in time
He learned to allow for its harsh effect
And came to see his striving and all the strain
Was meaningful. He felt everything added up—
He could not explain.

Often, Sunday afternoons, I see him with his little girl
Feeding crumbled bread to pigeons in the park
And if one comes to nibble from their hands,
They can't contain their laughter.
Then the pigeons scatter
And everyone around has to laugh too.

But everyone can't travel blind,
Find in himself cause enough to be and do
And project this upon events.
The resilient flesh that flinches yet accepts,
Offends some minds whose functioning depends
On pure and simple means to proud and proven ends—
I've seen a man stranded on the shore
Of his transcendent dream; he dared not stir
Lest circumstance corrupt and compromise

His sense of its direction.
I heard him say that revelation has its tide,
Would some day come sweeping in
And wash the stiffness from his limbs and then,
By God, he'd swim— he smiled at the image,
Said it justified his risk,
Standing there transfixed and out of reach.

V.
Balanced forces tend to immobility
But falling short, blend in modulated tides
Letting new and potent forms arise;
So the Hudson River, her deep and tranquil flowing,
Makes feasible the patterns of terrific enterprise
That crowd her shores and so aptly frames them
As to appease the trammeled eye.

My brother goes up in late spring
Into the High Sierras,
Through the silent sequoia stands and the pine,
Up to the treeless tors.
Sometimes he speaks about the Hudson,
Says the word, river,
Means always and only that river to him
And often he finds it flowing in his mind
Where it seems to correlate

The language of wonder and the language of daily use,
Images of the western ranges
And of the City in the east—
Say, a Mono Indian named Virgil
Whose silence is filled with the seasons of the forest
And the mountains' implacable shape,
And an old professor who failed to prove
His bold and faithful metaphysic
But did move his students sometimes
To look to the fundamental cause in things.
He confesses that his image of the river
Is both more and less than what the Hudson is,
But that by such correlations
And a kind of comprehensive laughter
He can relieve the stark discrepancy
Twixt what he dreams and what he does.

VI.
Overburdened by events observed
Or more obscurely sensed,
Slowly consciousness expands.
Too slow for measurement,
Too intricate and sudden
For immediate human demands.
Abruptly, consciousness contracts

As the quick, obliging flesh
Counteracts the subtle, self-losing mind.

I think there is a fertile brash conspiracy
That lets the city justify the river,
Astronomy arrange the stars and politicians
Take charge of all cosmic consequence:
If I laugh, I prove the jest.

In shafts of sunlight from slatted blinds,
Through whirling galaxies of dust,
I stray, a transparency to my own perception,
Spectrum of the fullness of the day.
Dusk; can be very quiet; the transitions;
In them half the meaning lies;
Let space be left for interpolations;
So vision opens into meta-vision
And then, with darkness, a decent ecstasy.

Thrust

Catch a comet's tail—
Let hands clench
Forever burning
In ever-thinning air;

Let hot stars blind
And the mind churn
In quicksands
Of boundless dark;

Let each hope die,
And dying be lonely
But let the trail blaze
Through earth's night,

If for a moment only,
Amaze and incite
Another soul to reach
For the comet's tail.

Toccata #2

Mounting fancies pantomime
The sloven pace, the awkward gauge
Of our far-fetched simianic race;

The brimful seed that binds to earth
Skyward tree and windward leaf,
Is burgeoning fancy's centerpiece

Whose growth-hush lingers in the ears,
Whose aerial crop lures grit-filled eyes,
Whose scent usurps the breath,

Is tonic, quickens the shamblefoot,
Flattens the belly, flings the arm.
Cries in the street swell to cantata:

Music measures sound. The trappings
Of the hero measure the man: he runs
And reaches out, he apes himself.

> Thus high holy days,
> Art and empire;
> Thus the gargoyle.

Understudy

I come as dolphin over leaping wastes
Of sea and seemingly in smiles and free
To deal with anyone whose skills and tastes
Allow that he may freely deal with me;

Or plunging into canyons undersea
To out-maneuver figments of the deep
And surge through mind-consuming density,
My mind and my survival in my keep;

The streams of blinding images that seep
Through consciousness I have no leave to spill,
For, mute but gleaming, from the world I reap
A dim applause, a semblance of good will.

And yet I would not play a dolphin's role
If I could find a part that used me whole.

The Unicorn Participates

I.

She walked across the Pont Neuf
And the proposition that came
From just behind, surprised her
For she had assumed she could go
Unnoticed—she quickened her pace,
The voice faded into the evening
And a rush of air wrapped itself
Around her as the last flames
Of sunset died out of the sky.

Wherever she walked
There lurked a unicorn,
Never clearly in sight,
Yet she was always aware
Of the lambent eye, the horn,
The swift, punishing hooves.

She walked along Wall Street
And in the dark silence her heels
Rang out against the pavement—
She would not look back in case
The tall façades that loomed
Towards her, seen sideways,
Should turn into a plantation

Of pale lines; her face burned
In the wind and she tasted brine.

She climbed up Russian Hill
And facing east, though sunrise
Was still an hour off, saw
That the sky was green; aware,
In a city heaving with sleep,
She had the world in her keeping:
A trust—but also an intrusion
For, being there, she denied it
Relief from what men make of it.

II.

To hold the world in one's hands,
To say to the world: Pumpkin,
Because of the long and short
Of my eyesight, the near and far
Of my hearing, the sharps and flats
Of my palate and nose, because
Of the thrills that run along my skin
Making the hairs standup,
I know that you are the magic coach…

To address the universe as pumpkin,
A growth, unitary, fluted,
Of such a muted orange tone;
To know it also as vehicle,

A contrivance, pieced, gilded,
On such high, spoked wheels;
In the face of oblivion to spin
The pumpkin, drive the coach,
To get it up the mountainside
And then, strength failing,
To watch as it slips, slides,
And goes crashing down again,
To watch without needing to force
A smile, without needing to pretend
That from the start, of course,
One had known the task were vain
And so had put no heart in it—
Nor to mock that figure
Down there, the figure of someone
Who bends over the debris
As if he might have found in it
The stuff of a new cosmos...

One may attribute much
To the promptings of the unicorn.

III.

She perches on a table and under her eye
The class constitutes itself:
        Out of shuffle and slouch,
        Scurry and stride,
        Angle and curve;
        Out of a sweep of faces,

112

Gaunt and round,

Blurred and bright,

Grimacing, deadpan,

With curtains of hair

Variously drawn;

Out of a flapping

Or clinging of garments,

And clutters and clutches

Of gear variously disposed…

When the class has compounded a body,

A body with a heavy, erratic pulse,

A body submerged in its own miasma,

In a dark pool dappled by expectation,

Eddied by distraction and dismay,

Stirred by currents of anger and desire,

A pool that threatens to engulf her,

That she may not withdraw from,

That she must plunge into,

Constructing channels,

Steering her course…

When the class has coalesced

And she is about to speak,

Then a second thought seizes her

And she gives it voice:

                    What if I say

That there is a unicorn in this room?

        Mr. Grey stares

        Miss Brown shrugs

        Miss Black looks bored

Mr. White rolls his eyes

Mr. Smith says: Are you putting us on?

What if I say

That there is always something unaccounted for
And perhaps unaccountable, in a room
Where people sit and play at cards
Or a solitary person stands
At the window looking down into the street
Or in a classroom where the discrepancy
That cannot be accounted for and the universe
That is unaccountable, may be summarized
As a unicorn lurking just out of sight
Or as a large pumpkin found on a doorstep...?
Think of it; think, then take up your pens;
Make something of it; make something good.

Mr. Grey goes blank

Miss Brown picks up a pen

Miss Black chews her beads

Mr. White leans his chin on his hand

Mr. Smith says: Give us another clue?

What if I say

That what we are, beyond what we seem,
What we feel, beyond what we can say,
Conjures up the pumpkin, summons
The unicorn and lends them force...?
Now let us see what you make of it.

Mr. Grey draws a stick figure
With a pumpkin head...

Miss Brown writes: There is no
Such thing as a unicorn…
Miss Black writes: This kind
Of assignment is not fair…
Mr. White draws a unicorn
Bow-legged and fat
Mr. Smith writes: If you say
There is a unicorn in this room
I suppose you must believe
Such a being or beast,
Or at least such a smell
Is here in this room:
Your nose, your belief, your unicorn –
But leave the pumpkin out of it.
Nothing is plainer than pumpkins.
Every year, come fall, I single out
A pumpkin that is solid and symmetrical
And summarize it as a Jack O'Lantern;
All I need is a look at it
And a heft of it, a small amount
Of hard cash and a sharp knife.

As for unicorns, I think I am willing
To see one—but I don't.
I think I am willing to recognize
The smell of one—but I can't.
I think I am willing—maybe I'm not.
Maybe I want a world as solid,
Symmetrical and plain as a pumpkin is.

Maybe I want to shut out
What I cannot put into words,
The sudden warping of a room,
The look behind the look on a face,
The echo that should not be there—

                              What is the blur,
Wavering and white, there,
In the back of the room?
I can see it from the corner of my eye.
I can almost make out a curling mane.
I can almost make out a shining horn.
Why should my eyes smart?
Why should my neck feel stiff?
Maybe I should turn around to look
But

                              Time is up.

IV.

A park, late in October;
A sun sinking, pale;
Red and gold of leaves,
Muted; grass, tarnished;
Mr. Smith, a pumpkin
Tucked underarm, climbs
A bald hill; no one
Else in sight; reaches
The top, sits; places
Pumpkin before him, takes
Knife from pocket, traces

A Jack O'Lantern face;
Looks at it—it is right;
Cuts circular section
From top of pumpkin, scoops out
Pulp and seeds; then
Cuts out as traced, two eyes
And a nose and a gap-toothed
Gash for a grinning mouth;
Sets his handiwork before him—
It is what he's had in mind.
Mutters: A fig for unicorns …
Wipes, puts away his knife;
Rises, stretches; lifts
Pumpkin, cradles it in his arms;
Starts down the hill slowly—
Gains momentum, loping,
Then, galloping: trips,
Falls, the fruit of his labor
Under him, Jack-face
Smash against stony ground.

Mr. Smith sits up,
In the last light of the day
Studies the work of his hands:
It is beyond repair—
DAMN THAT UNICORN,
Cries Mr. Smith.

V.

She is drawn to the window one night
By the sound of a passerby whistling.
She peers into darkness broken
By patches of lamp light and sees
On the near side of the street,
Mr. Smith, whistling.
She smiles and draws back
Into the shadow of the unlit room…

To hear a tune whistled
In the night, to have it nip
One's mind like a warm wind
With a cold edge, a wind
Sharpened by one's own movement,
To identify the source of the sound
And be content to let it pass…

To bear oneself as vehicle,
A patchwork of moving parts,
Lurching to an end that is universal
Along a path that is unique
In a service at once obvious and obscure;
But also to bear oneself as the fruit
Of an ancient, prolific vine,
All of a piece, rounded,
With a surface on which several faces

May have been traced, but one
Only will have been carved…

The unicorn, out of sight
Or lurking and lashing out
With sharp hooves, in all this
Plays a crucial part.

View from a Barge on the Nile

c. 1358 B.C.

"…There, in the east, first light, soft;

Now, in its wake, rises the Sun.

Dog-headed baboons begin to bark;

Lynx and braying ass stretch;

Quail and snipe scurry in the reeds;

Hippopotamus and crocodile stir in the mud;

Duck, heron and stork wheel overhead;

The pelican, steadfast upon her nest,

Preens herself and her breast is stained

With the sanguine light. In dense fields

Of barley, wheat or spelt, in vineyards,

In groves of date-palm and in coves

Where fishnets are kept, the copper-skinned,

The credulous men of Egypt pause

And give praise to the Sun whose ascendant rays

Drive off the night-infesting shapes of dread

And stay the pangs of mortality.

"The waters of Nile are tinged with flame;

Gently my barge sways. At my left

Foaming beer is set and such

Barley cakes and choice honeycombs

As are placed in tombs and offered in temples;

At my right, fresh papyrus scrolls.

But I that was chief of Pharaoh's scribes,

And diligent, now Pharaoh is dead,

Ride at anchor under a canopy

And brood; eat and drink at whim—
Brush away a buzzing fly.
It persists, I catch and crush it, wipe
And fold my hands. Pharaoh dead,
Who turned his people toward the Sun,
Saying: think on this life;
Rejoice in its source; love Him;
Saying: let there be in Egypt
No other gods, for only the Sun
Is everywhere plain to our sense.
And now Egypt hastens to restore
Her motley gods, yet the Sun
That should have come up in a pall of dust
And could have laid all Egypt waste,
Rises undimmed, quickens the land,
Wakens and warms man and beast.
Even though Pharaoh praised One,
He died and his labor shall be undone;
And though Egyptians praise many,
They toil and die, are maimed in battle,
Suffer plagues and the sting of the scorpion;
And their women die in childbirth although
They have made unusual offerings to Isis…
Indeed, if Isis and Osiris, Apis,
Thoth, Amon-Aten and the rest
Be something more than names men make
For tides that sweep, subside and sweep
Again our shallows and our deeps—indeed,
If the gods be, surely they care

No more for men than men for flies,

Love Egypt no more than Egypt loves

Distant savage tribes. Or

If the gods be and care at all,

It is only insofar as they may use us

To ends that are not ours—so,

Heedless of our praise or pleading, they shape

To their measure our coinciding world.

"...Now the Sun is high and the silence

And heat wash and weight the scene;

No creature stirs; no shadow is cast;

The pelican's head is under her wing...

But stillness is nothing new to me

For, although in the presence of Pharaoh

There was always talk and often music,

And when courtiers and councilors were dismissed,

The ibis-necked, the gentle queen

Remained and often the royal daughters,

One or both, at her side, playing,

And always attendants and guards at the portals,

And some further call for my scrolls...

Yet, before morning, I would return

To my father's empty house and there

Stillness prevailed, for my father lay

In his tomb with his stone image and his scarabs,

His throwing sticks and his court robes

And all the marks of his rank in order,

As they say, to be well-received by Osiris.

Yes, my father, who was pious, died
At the start of Pharaoh's reign, and before him,
His barren sister-wife, who was mild
As the gazelle, collared in gold and amethyst,
She gave me in my childhood—it lived a while
In our garden; and the great cypress there,
Where the hoopoes used to gather noisily,
That tree has fallen; and my own mother,
My father's concubine, died at my birth;
And my nurse, too, in spite of her amulets
Against every possible bane; and my tutor
(Sometimes at night I secretly watched
As he drank his wine and silently wept);
And the great wily hunting cat,
Collared in jaspar and gold, we used,
My father and I, in the game-rich marshes;
And companions of my youth—yes, my cousin,
Who, after a voyage we made together
In foreign ships, set out once more,
Alone, for barbaric lands and vanished;
And a wasting sickness fell upon my wife,
Driving her beyond the reach of my voice,
Out of the hands of doctors and priests,
Against her will, into the house of death.
In time, even the sorrowful shadow
She left in my care, had passed away...
All of them, gone, and now Pharaoh, too,
And overhead the Sun, a blazing stone,

Is held to its distant, westward course
As little aware of why as we.

"...The waters of the Nile ripple and shift;
My barge sways. On the shores of the river,
In the fields, in kitchens and temples and shops,
The people of Egypt make ready against the night.
I perceive their urgency; it leaves me untouched.
Pomegranates and figs have been set before me,
Nutmeats and wine. I sip the wine:
It quenches and in quenching stirs the appetites.
I sip and savor it and even in solitude,
Idle, aging, account each moment
Death is deferred, dear in itself,
For the moment afterwards may see me stripped
Of sense and senses, at one with the multitudes
In the dim, stale house of death,
With those who, thoughtless or thoughtful, denied
And those who only thought to please
The gods and in giving death's estate
The gear and semblance of life, sought
Transcendence of the brute design that binds
The joys we know and all our knowing
To quickness of flesh—or resigned themselves
To loss of self and consoled themselves
In saying: though each Egyptian dies,
Egypt lives, renewed in our progeny,
And the gods of Egypt live forever...
But in the evening air is the smell of carrion

124

And I think already Egypt decays
And in time the pyramids will turn to dust
And the names of the gods will be forgotten,
And someday the Nile will dry in her bed
And, at last, the Sun will not rise
And we will be one with the dust and the darkness,
Unremembered and indifferent. Where is the proof
Of immortality, where the binding need for it?
A wind stirs, a stone bursts into flame,
Crosses the sky—its heat and light
Bake and split the dust, something flows,
The river, then grasses and trees, beasts
And man and he builds his cities until
The recurrent stone begins to cool,
As even the hottest embers will and the world
Crumbles, and as if a great wind
Had passed, there is surpassing stillness.
So be it. I did not see its coming
And surely I will not see its going;
It is good to be mortal in a mortal world.

"... There, in the west, last light, soft;
   Now, in the east, darkness, and stars
   Beyond counting, slowly shifting,
   Pattern the sky—one star falls. Wind,
   Fitful and chill, rustles in the reeds,
   Carries the cry of a night-bird, pauses;
   Waves slap at the side of the barge
   And her timbers creak; from the farther shore

Drifts the sound of sistrum and flute,
Recalling images of adventure and opulence—
Another star falls—the life I have lived
And the life I have dreamt of merge in the night's
Largesse that holds time in suspense,
Quelling regrets and the fear of death—
Is it brilliance or darkness that stops my breath?
Or an omen, the third star falling, and now,
Perfect stillness and a shower of stars."

Week-Song

Like wind and the river,
Life is swift is slow
And only seven days pass
Between birth and dying.

The house we happen into,
The house we build,
Knowing, or not,
Is kept by seven days
That take us round on round.

Motley in their gifts,
Much-used, they are harlots
Who, eyes like river-eddies,
Smile on all comers loosely,

In turn, preside at table,
Deal fortunes from an ancient pack,
Like wind, flicking cards,
Themselves, unmoved,
They take their fees.

Then, in the night, silent,
Each one passes to the one
Who comes after her
Keys that open every door.

And briefly their figures,
Posturing, buxom or lean,
Caught in lamp or moonlight,
Cast shadows of opulence
On the walls and the floors.

The White Steed

1. The white steed speeds
   Across what remains
   Of the western plain;
   White, with a wild mane
   In a whirling of wind—
   Hot breath cleaving
   A whole, cold air,
   Or a wind of itself wild,
   A hurtling of air, air-driven.

2. The white marble steed
   Of the Parthenon frieze,
   Broader in chest,
   Higher at shoulder, holds
   His summary stance—
   The galloping horse contracts,
   Harder, whiter in the wind
   On the lessening plain
   And, headlong, irresistible.

3. The white steed stops short
   As if suddenly corralled,
   Tests the unbridled wind,
   Breathes his own sweat,
   Paws the ground—then rears,
   Breaks halt, hurtles
   Across the shifting plain,
   Careless how fast or far he goes
   And where, at last, he falls.

Willow Patterns

Dried willows
　　Cut in spring
　　　　Last for months,
　　　　　　In lamplight cast
　　　　　　　　Pleasing shadows
　　　　　　　　　　Upon a bare wall.
You called that wasteful—
If it lay in my hands, you said,
To root them and let them grow
You'd take them for planting
　　　　　　So I placed the branches
　　　　　　In a bucket of water and cared
　　　　　　For them until they quickened—
Now pale root-tendrils reach
For earth-hold, the catkins
Have begun to pollenate
And new leaves are sprouting
　　　　　　You should have come for them
　　　　　　Last week—soon the leaves
　　　　　　Will wither, the roots, decay.
　　Damp willow
　　　　Chokes the fire,
　　　　　　Is slow-burning
　　　　　　　　And live wood
　　　　　　　　　　Smokes, turning
　　　　　　　　　　　　The eyes to water.

Word-Play

If words rang true in the wind
And not in the treacherous ear
Alone, then words would be one
With the wind, as often they are
Insofar as ears may be deaf.

--Chrysostomos, master of words,
Was heard in his time by multitudes;
Now in our ears there lingers
The sound of his name alone:
The golden flight of his words,
Waylaid by the winds of time,
Is merged in the glow of the crocus,
Dispersed in the slipstreams of fall.

II.

If domesticity abhors a paradox
(Creeping things that cannot be caught,
Or time's disproof: excess of logic)
And poetry abhors a cliché (say,
That a rose is a rose: excess of use),
Let the housewife learn to brush off words
And the poet to be dismayed by threadbare
Furnishings: a reversal, upon my word,

That gives grounds for a meeting of minds,
Almost, for a marriage of many conveniences.

--But if a word can split a hair,
A sentence, cut off a head, and the terms
Of a deadman's will bind his heirs,
Then hold the tongue that pulls apart
What had been whole, or agglutinates
What had kept itself to itself and moved
As it listed, without any strings attached.

III.

If wisdom shaped up as a pearl does,
Or a pig, had luster, therefore, or smell
(The smell of bacon sizzling on a grill),
Then wisdom in some degree would weigh,
As it often does, with pigs or pig iron,
Iron ore, oriental pearls or pure
Oil of olives, and corner markets.
There's a course for you: render wisdom;
Extract function, formula and fact;
Trade for unction, rank and rule.

--Consider Gentle Ascham who could loose
The arrow of a thought in so high an arc
That till it hit, none could tell
What its target was: it was fit his discourse
On archery should win Royal Henry's pension,
At university and court, even a summons

From Henry's quick-witted, red-haired child
To come, teach her classic tongues
And the princely style in homely speech.

And if wisdom refused ever to pluck
Fortune's sleeve or put on fancy dress
Or sing for a supper, if wisdom refused
To squeeze laughter from stone-sober
Thought, it might well remain a closed book.

--When Elizabeth (the massive fleet of Spain
Bearing down on her) told her men
She had the heart and stomach of a king
And a king of England at that, the men
Said they'd die for her: did she recall
Ascham's insistence that manner was all?
And admiring her rhetoric, her acute ear
For the earthy support a royal stomach
Must lend to a royal heart, do we
Applaud the tutor with the Tudor queen?

IV.

For all their fertile opulence,
For all their willfulness and guile,
For all their splendid alliances,
Cleopatra and Alianor would fade
With the fading effects of their actions
If not for the eloquence they inspired:
Even the rose has been glorified

In respect of such royal women,
Figuratively, and overblown.

--Yet around the world the roses
Grow in petaled profusion,
As lovely in scent and hue,
As golden and opaque at heart,
As thorny-stemmed as ever,
And as tempting to the worm.

V.

Call up legendary names;
Pay homage to flowers; hurl
Words against the wall of time,
Stack them in tunnels of vacancy,
Set them as steps going in
And out of perilous gorges,
Weave of them collars and leashes
And lead forth monsters;
Cross a page with trains
Of phrases (tooled and retooled,
Oiled and wiped) from sidetracks
Of the mind; make game
Of all deep cravings,
Even the craving to speak
And be heard, to take the word
From a place in nature, to play with it

As so much of the dark

And so much of the light;

Make sport of such an art,

Borrow another name for it:

Call it strip-poker

Or blindman's bluff, backgammon

Or hide-and-seek, call it

Ring-around-a-rosy.

Words on Music?

For C. Raney

When it comes to music, Lady, let me be mute.
Let me be silent about how the player should play,
About the concepts informing the piece, what it means,
What we mean by meaning in music—

                        Surrounded by sound,
Let me surrender. Let it fill the spaces in me
That wait to be filled. Music that finds,
Binds me in terms of its own. Let me avoid
Putting this into words—

                  Lady, it is enough
That I talk of literature and of art, of the craft
That unifies a work, and try to explain
How form and content, that seem to interact,
Are two views of one thing—

                  I must speak
Of poems, point out sounds that repeat,
Vary and repeat, imagery that recurs,
The beat, ambiguous or marked, that bind
The ear, the eye, the mind—

                  I must speak
Of the point the poem makes, and try to explain
That the point is not the poem, that patterned sound
And pointed meaning do not account for lines

That seize the mind and hold—

                    Like those of Yeats:

"Their eyes mid many wrinkles, their eyes,

Their ancient, glittering eyes, are gay"…

Why these lines so intensely please, at the end

Of "Lapis Lazuli"—

                 I cannot explain,

But as I picture the old men listening, there,

On the hillside, to the music their servant plays,

I imagine that they may delight in the scene

And the sound, Lady,

                  Because they must be mute.

These poems have been published earlier:

1. "Toccata"—an early version of "Toccata #2," included here—in ZERO, Winter 1950, vol. 1, #3/4

2. "Paean" in ZERO, June 1954, vol. 2, #5

3. "Blindman's Bluff" in "Riverside Poetry 2," 1956

4. "Et Ego, Mr. Eliot?" in Zero, spring 1956, vol. w, #7

5. "Soliloquy" in "Quixote" in spring 1958

6. "Interregnum #1, "Interregnum #2" and "Interregnum #3 in "The Notre Dame English Journal," Winter 1967/68

7. "Birdscapes" in "The Maryland Institute Quarterly Newsletter," Spring 1970, vol. 7, #3

8. "Extractions" in "The Paper," Dec. 1970/January 1971

9. "The Unicorn Participates" in "The American Association of University Professors Bulletin," March 1974, vol. 17, #1

10. "Letter from Kyoto" in "Caim," Fall 1975, vol. 2, #2

11. "Words on Music?" in "The college Music Symposium," Spring 1977, vol. 17, #1

12. "Soliloquy," republished by "Gulp!," December 1977

13. "Set Piece" and "August #2 in POETRY AT THE ANGEL, an anthology, 1978

14. "Meditation at a Window" in "The Ear's Chamber," Scop V 1981

15. "Ballad" in "Influence," June-July 1988, Vol. 1

16. "Ab Ovo" in "Influence," August-September 1988, vol. 1

Jean Rubin was born in New York City in 1928. She received a B.A. from Smith College in 1948 and an M.A. from Columbia University in 1957, both degrees in English. Also in 1957, a manuscript of her poems was a finalist in the Yale Younger Poets competition.

In 1963 her poem, "Theme and Variations," was co-winner of a Robert Frost Award from the Poetry Society of America.

In 1976, she created for the composer, Robert Hall Lewis, a text that he used to structure his "Combinazioni III for Oboe/English Horn, Percussion, and Narrator." This was subsequently performed in Carnegie Hall's Weill Recital Hall in New York City, and also at Goucher College and Peabody Conservatory in Baltimore.

She held various jobs in New York and San Francisco until she came to Baltimore in 1962 to join the faculty of the Maryland Institute, College of Art, where she taught writing and Literature until she retired in 1990. She still lives in Baltimore.

At about the age of nine, she came across a photograph of the Taj Mahal. She had already spent a summer in Belgium, and now knew that she would have to go to India. In 1965, she did so, on her way from England to Japan—she had made earlier voyages to several European countries and would do so again, afterward.

For more information on Jean Rubin's work log on to:
www.boudicapublishing.com

Boudica Publishing Inc.

Publishes progressive fiction and non-fiction and features the imprints:

Wildfire Poetry Press

LESBIAN MYSTERY BOOKS

www.boudicapublishing.com

Made in the USA
Middletown, DE
31 January 2023

23603985R00086